A Short History of Mississippi Coast Gambling

Told by one who worked it.

By Hank Roberts

Story by Hank Roberts
© Hank Roberts - 2019
All Rights Reserved

Edited by Philip Levin
Published by Doctor's Dreams
PO Box 4808
Biloxi, MS 39535
www.Doctors-Dreams.com
writerpllevin@gmail.com

No part of this production may be reproduced, stored in a retrieval system, or transmitted in any form or by any means, electronic, mechanical, recording, or otherwise, without the prior permission of the author.

Prepared in the United States of America
ISBN: 978-1-942181-14-9

A Short History of Mississippi Coast Gambling

Hank Roberts

CHAPTER ONE

It was a cold and dreary night in the middle of January, 1964, when the Boss sent me and three other hoods down to the French Quarter. There was a convention going on in a ritzy hotel and our job was to set up a craps game. We're talking big money conventions with gold-watch lawyers, all ready to throw their money around to impress the ladies and each other. Barely eighteen-years-old, this was my first gig, though I'd heard about these "bar associations," where the fellows enjoyed their gambling, booze, and women. No bet was too high, nor was any woman too expensive once the lawyers had a few drinks under their belt.

Anyone who has lived through a winter in New Orleans knows how the moisture blowing off the waters penetrates to your bones. As we got out of our chauffeured big black car, we heard the crisp crack of a pistol firing in the distance. I glanced at Bulldog, our overseer, who just shrugged. After all, we were in New Orleans, the murder capital of the country. Shivering from the cold more than the gunshot, we hurried into the hotel.

The craps table had already been set up by some other hoods and they'd spread the word. Besides the lawyers, other would-be millionaires with foolish visions of grandeur drew to the fire like moths, convinced they'd make money off the gambling bosses. However, the house never lost. We always walked away with much more winnings than any of the players.

There were four of us, one stick man, two dealers and Bulldog. When pompous blowhards began losing, they'd occasionally get rowdy. Bulldog kept a 38-revolver showing behind his coat lapel as a reminder of who was in control. When he told the gamblers his name was Bulldog, he explained they should come to him if they needed anything. He let them know he could be their best friend ... or their worst enemy. I made a point of staying on his good side, never asking anything of him. I figured it was best to let a sleeping dog lie.

Since I was very new at this sort of activity, I had many questions about how this all worked, questions that remained unasked and unanswered. I was afraid to ask the big bosses anything and didn't ask my fellow thugs because I didn't want to appear dumb.

I figured time and experience would be the greatest teachers.

Before this gig the bosses made sure I knew two things: the rules of craps, such as the bets and payoffs, and second, how to protect myself and the table winnings. The bosses frowned at anyone returning from a game having lost their winnings. Some players, called skaggs, would purposely try to disrupt a game or cheat. There were always dummies who thought they were stronger and smarter than the house. However, they usually got caught, and when they did, the bosses' strong arms would make a spectacle of the revenge. I learned quickly that the mob was not a bad bunch to work for as long as one didn't try to cross 'em.

As the night went on, more and more players drifted in to join the game, squeezing into the small room. Ashes piled on the floor and the air fogged with smoke. We kept a small fan blowing over the table so we could see the bets and dice rolls. With the four of us eye-hawking the table, we made sure no one skimmed any money. Every few hours the two dealers would switch out.

The booze flowed freely. Some of the gamblers would come to the table already drunk, but even if they weren't drunk when they got there, as soon as they had started placing their bets they'd partake of the free drinks we offered. I got the willies seeing how much booze they were drinking. Any real gambler knew they shouldn't drink, or at least not get drunk, while he was at the table and wagering. Bulldog was always happy to see that all gamblers had all they wanted to drink. A drunk player tended to place foolish and higher bets. Unlike locals, convention goers seemed a completely different breed. They didn't seem to mind losing their money, especially if they had a girl in one hand and a drink in the other.

Though I was young and inexperienced, I realized right away it was best to follow the rules. Gambling was easy for the bosses to monitor. There were four of us at the table, all of whom kept their eyes on the intake, payouts, and each other. Even the tips were placed in a common fund. The Boss would make sure we got a fair payout at the end.

However, some of the other activities weren't so easy to monitor. The Boss made sure there was a pimp to help the conventioneers have plenty of ladies. The pimp was supposed to keep track of how many times a working girl was rented out on any particular night. If the pimp didn't report all the transactions with the idea that maybe he could skim off some of the Boss's money, he just might end up taking a long walk off a New Orleans' short pier.

Like the whores, the drugs were difficult to keep track of. Sometimes a dealer thought he could be smart by cutting the stash with starch and selling a weaker line in order to skim money from the sales. If the customers caught on, they'd complain, and word would get back to the Boss. Once again, it could end up with a fellow wearing concrete shoes in the river.

However, for the most part, everyone who worked for the Boss played it straight and we rarely heard of one of the gang being offed. Stories about a New York or Chicago mob wiping out many of their competitors, and sometlme even themselves, circulated through the clubs but didn't concern us much. We were one happy family, so to speak.

    Back to the game at the hotel. About 2 a.m. one of the guests got so drunk that he began questioning the calls on the table. Since I was the stickman on the table, he was basically questioning me. Bulldog stepped up to him and reminded him that he should be nice if he wanted to play on our game. The man made a very poor decision. He took a punch at Bulldog. Bulldog used his slapjack to knock the player to the ground and kept him there with the barrel of a pistol pointed at his noggin. The guy was pouring out blood, and so, with an ambulance on the way, the four of us gathered up our cash and faded off into the night. Back at the Club we handed over our takings and received our pay for our evening's work.

I liked my job. The pay was good and the work easy. Yeah, technically, gambling was illegal, but in "The Big Easy" the law looked the other way. It was just something that was carried out without much attention. I figured the government officials were paid kickbacks from the gambling operations, so everyone was happy. Heck, one of the big reasons conventions came here was because everyone knew about the gambling. No one seemed to mind, even the victims, because, after all, it was their choice to give us money for a bit of a good time.

The Boss had a big region. By the time I turned twenty, I had become quite good at my job and was being used to work from New Orleans to Biloxi. This covered a wide spectrum of places and a large variety of types of joints. Some of the small joints were nothing more than a bar and a bathroom. Sometimes there would be a small out-back room where card games were played. These establishments were no place for the weak of heart or stomach. Often fights would break out where people might lose teeth, an eye, or even their life. One joint displayed a man's ear that had been cut off during a fight in the joint. It was nailed to the wall for everyone to see. I sometimes wondered if it was there to brag or to deter people from fighting.

    Most of these small locations were patrolled by the individual sheriff departments of the residing parish or county. If someone was beaten badly, the law might or might not show up. The victims usually had to manage to find their own way home. A patron of any of these joints had to keep two things in mind: no cheating at cards and no stealing another man's woman. Although most of the women weren't dazzling beauties, to put it mildly, nevertheless they were actively defended by their men. Of course, you could buy one of these girls from her man, especially if he was losing at cards, but you would be well advised not to try to steal her.

On one occasion a guy known as Crabby was drinking heavily and playing cards in the back room. Another man came into the front door and saw Crabby's woman sitting alone at the bar. The newcomer rambled up to the woman and asked if he could buy her a drink. She accepted. After a couple more drinks, the two of them slipped out the front door and into the newcomer's car. A few minutes later,

Crabby, who'd lost all his cash, came out to take his girl home. The barkeep told him that she had stepped out with another man. Crabby walked outside and spotted condensation building up on the windows of a green Volvo parked on the side of the building. Going to the trunk of his own car, Crabby took out an ax, and held it behind his back as he went up to the Volvo and knocked on the window. When the man opened the door, Crabby sunk the ax into the man's skull. When the police arrived, Crabby told them exactly what had happened. He told the cops he figured he'd have to spend some time in jail, but had decided it was worth it.

Louisiana seemed to have more wealthy gamblers than Mississippi. These local Cajun gamblers were often ready to put their fortunes on the line and there was always an organized gambler willing to take it.

    The Spot was a medium size nightclub located on the highway just east of New Orleans and just before the Mississippi State line. There were several intersecting highways that came into Highway 90 close to the Spot, highways built especially for the nightclub, thanks to contributions given by the gambling organizations to the Louisiana Highway Department and the Governor's office. This place was properly named because it was the spot where everything happened, the business center of the area's bosses. Tales were told of people losing homes, property, boats, and large sums of money there at the Spot.

    The Spot was one of the first establishments to possess penny, nickel, and quarter slot machines. In those days, the machines took coins in and paid out in coin cash. With its restaurant serving pretty good food, men would bring their ladies there for a meal, and after eating, the women would play the slots while the men would drift off to the card room. The Spot grew so large that it soon had a dance floor with live bands. It was widely known for the ladies that worked there, although they tried to be discreet so as not to drive off the "proper" ladies who came with their escorts.

    Several times I was asked to go there to work, sometimes for as long as a week. Once I was sitting with a county alderman and his wife. We were having dinner in the restaurant when another government official came in with a lovely lady on his arm. Amy, the wife of the alderman that I was dining with, knew the government official who had just come in.

"That's not his wife," Amy whispered. She nudged her husband. "John, do you know who that woman is?"

John took a quick glance and said, matter-of-factly, "That's his mistress."

Amy was aghast. "Why that's awful! A government man shouldn't have a mistress."

John pulled out his wallet and pulled out a picture of a beautiful woman he showed to Amy. "This is my mistress," he told her.

Amy's mouth dropped open. "John! What are you saying?"

"Oh, don't make a scene. It's a status symbol to have a mistress around here. You want me to keep getting elected? I have to have a mistress."

Amy picked up the photo and compared it to the woman that had just come in.

She nodded in appreciation. "Well, clearly you're doing better than him. His mistress isn't nearly as pretty as ours!"

I laughed so hard my gin and tonic came spewing out my nose.

The owner of the Spot became so successful that he began setting up joints all along the Mississippi Coast. Some places were known to have gambling, and some had working ladies of the night. Some establishments catered to large dance halls and restaurants where famous performers would come and make a hefty profit for the managers. The smaller joints often turned to striptease acts and depended on the money made from their girls. Some of the joints also sold drugs on the side, but that was not a common thing since they were selling so much booze they didn't need the extra headaches of illegal drugs.

   I happened to be visiting one of the small joints one night, a place known for its beautiful strippers. I knew all the girls, as well as the owner, Toes Jones. What I didn't know, though, was that Toes was selling drugs on the side. On this night, two men came in and asked for Toes to step outside with them to discuss some business. A few minutes later I heard a loud scream and then six pistol shots. Everyone in the bar hid under the tables until we figured the hit men had driven off, and then I peeked out. There I found Toes with a hatchet driven through his right shoe and six bullet holes, one of which was right through his forehead. I heard later that he had been skimming money and the Boss had found out.

One police car came with the coroner, but the officer didn't ask for witnesses and we all kept quiet.

Personally, I never was concerned about my own safety. I always figured if I played it straight and stuck with the hotel gambling business, I wouldn't have to worry.

CHAPTER TWO

Because it was the largest and most active of all the gambling halls, I'd often work at the Spot. I would deal cards, manage the craps table, and sometimes, against my preference, I would be asked to run the Wheel of Fortune. This was a vertical wheel with a table in front of it for gamblers to place their bets. Usually this game was run by a lovely lady, however, if all the ladies were busy with customers, I would be called upon to take over. Because I didn't have the, um, physical equipment that attracted the men, I'd never bring in as much money as the women.

The call girls could bring in large sums of money for the bosses. The customers could pay small amounts for a quick trick, or larger amounts for a longer time, even an all-nighter. Some girls, called "B drinkers," simply worked the bar. Their job was to get the customers to buy them drinks. Booths were set up in dark places for the girls to take generous customers. The B-drinkers were not allowed to take customers to the rooms. That was reserved for the trained prostitutes. However, a lot could be done in the dark booth, if the customer was willing to pay.

In order to keep the B-drinkers from becoming drunk, they were fed sticks of butter before their work started. This would coat the upper part of their stomachs and slow down the alcohol absorption. Also, the bartenders knew to water down the girls' drinks. The customer didn't care as long as he got what he wanted.

In the back room of the Spot were three blackjack tables, one large poker table, a craps table and the Wheel. These table games attracted masses of active gamblers. It was one of the few places with a variety of games. Since the law officers were paid to look the other way, there was no worry about being busted. Occasionally the Sheriff's deputies would stop in and walk around, just so they would be seen. The spotter outside would inform us when the police arrived so we could close the Wheel, which was the only obvious gambling device, everything else just being tables. The police would take their time getting out of their car and coming in. Though they'd never actually ask for it, one of them would pass by the bar where the bartender would slip him a small envelope. Then the police would walk around, say hello to those they knew, and politely leave, having assured everyone that there was no obvious gambling going on.

There was always one informant on the city council or board of directors of the county. These insiders would warn in advance when the police were planning a raid on any of the establishments. In this way, all the gaming material could be dismantled and stored away. The back rooms would just look like large dance floors, where a jukebox generally stood in the corner. Sometime a couple of slot machines were confiscated just so it looked like a real raid. Pictures were taken of the police destroying the machines for use in the newspapers. This was great press for the ultra-conservative ladies of the various communities.

    The bosses were too rich and too smart to allow government officials to interrupt organized gaming. Illegal booze was shifted from one place to another.

Ladies of the night were promptly bailed out of jail. The only thing that was not tolerated by the law was illegal drugs. The joints that did deal in drugs had to pay much more hush money to the officials to keep their eyes shut and their mouths closed.

The Spot did not allow drug trafficking. They were making too much money to allow the dangers of that business. Besides, the operators of the joints that did sell drugs were totally satisfied with the Spot staying out of that business.

Since the Spot was so successful, the Boss decided to expand into Biloxi, Mississippi. He established a couple of clubs along Highway 90, also known as Beach Boulevard, because, well, it ran along the beach. Over a period of two to three years, these clubs built up a reputation for having great entertainers, booze, gambling, girls, good food, and sometimes illegal drugs. Several of the club owners from Louisiana moved over to the Mississippi Gulf Coast and established their own popular businesses. It was very difficult for the untrained eye to know which of the clubs were fronts for illicit activities and which ones were legitimately run by the large group of financiers in Dixie.

Biloxi became known to all of Mississippi's convention goers. Highway

90 in Biloxi became known as the "Golden Strip." When large limousines came to town bringing nationally known entertainers, even the locals would turn out. Some wealthy businessmen from New Orleans came to the Mississippi Coast and set up legitimate restaurants and motels. Tourists could sunbathe on the thirty miles of white sand beaches, liquor flowing freely in the bars, and great entertainers performing in fine nightclubs. Who could ask for anything more?

In one of the newly formed clubs, I learned one of the greatest lessons of my life. There was a man, "Deadeye" was his name, who ran the roulette wheel. He was the only one allowed to spin the wheel. We became friends and would often have chats over a cup of coffee during our breaks. I asked him why he was the only one allowed to run roulette. He said he could spin the wheel and release the steel ball in such a way as to make it hit on any number that he wanted. Deadeye would see where the bets were placed and then he would roll the ball so that it would land on a number where there were no bets. I called BS on that. He bet me my entire week's pay that we could go to the wheel and I could name three numbers, one at a time, and he could roll each individually. That seemed impossible. It would be difficult to roll any exact number, let alone three times in a row. I took his bet.

   We proceeded to a roulette wheel which had been closed during his break. Deadeye spun the wheel and asked me for my first number. After I gave it to him, he began studying the turning wheel. With his fingers he slowed the wheel to exactly the speed he wanted. He then waited for my number to get right under his finger and he let go of the steel ball. The ball rotated around the rim, in the opposite direction from the wheel. As the ball dropped down and bounced around, it settled right into the number that I had chosen. Wow!! What a talent. I still didn't believe that he could do this three times in a row. I picked out two more numbers, well-spaced from each other. He spun the wheel two more times. Each time the ball fell into the exact number that I had chosen. I was heartbroken, but I readily gave him the amount of our bet.

He looked at me and said, "I'm going to give you some good advice. Never bet against a man on his own game. People will not hustle you if they don't know for certain that they can win. Consider the ball under the nutshell, or the three playing cards that are mixed up after showing you one of them. These people know exactly what they can do with their game and you will never win."

CHAPTER THREE

There were rivers of booze that flowed through the many joints located on the Gulf Coast. Because Mississippi had no Alcohol Beverage Commission at that time, the only things regulating the liquor flow were who had the largest bankroll and who had the biggest gun. It didn't take long for a couple of kingpins to realize that they would become very wealthy if they could corner the alcohol market. Two bosses decided to do just that. First, they had to secure the source of purchases. Second, they had to have room to store all the booze that came onto the Coast.

The source of supply of the liquor was readily secured when the bosses sent four muscle men to meet with the various alcohol brand dealers. The muscle men made it quite clear that the booze salespersons were to sell only to the organized bosses. The salesmen would make the same amount of money, and they would have ready sales for their wares. For them it was a winning situation. No more calls on small joints and no more hassles with orders that would not produce a large profit. Perhaps it helped that a bit of the persuasion included looking down the barrels of sawed-off shotguns.

    Next came the job of finding enough storage to house all the liquor that was coming in. It turned out that one of the hotels in Biloxi had a large facility located in the far back of their property. Additions were made to this facility, making it the perfect location. It was off the beaten path and the access roads were closed to unwanted traffic. The bosses were pleased with the site and the completed arrangements. The hotel, for its cooperation, found itself with a brand-new swimming pool for its guests. Everyone seemed to be happy.

Next the syndicate announced that liquor would only be available through the warehouse. Orders could be taken and the goods delivered only through known employees of the Boss. This created new jobs: there had to be agents visiting joints and taking orders and there had to be truck drivers to deliver the hooch. There were a few joint owners who complained at first about the set cost of the booze. After one of their joints burned to the ground with its owner inside, the cooperation from the other owners became very smooth. The clubs that had B drinkers were made to purchase more liquor because the watered-down drinks for the girls was not using enough alcohol to support those clubs' existence. Except for the occasional gruesome demonstration, all-in-all everything ran very smoothly.

There was a definite pecking order to the entire organization and everyone knew their place. No one tried to step up, and certainly no one wanted to step down. There was enough booze, girls, and blow to go around for everyone. Gambling still took the front seat to all other ventures. The dealers knew one another and they all, whether they liked it or not, got along with each other. New clubs opened and new gambling joints popped up. There were even card games conducted in private homes and at apartment complexes. The operators of these private games did not have to ask permission from the bosses to run their activities. They did, however, greet the bosses' representatives when they made surprise visits. There would always be a small envelope containing cash that would be slipped to them for a gratitude gesture to the Boss.

In downtown Biloxi there was a club that was the hub of local gambling. There were card tables, slot machines, and bookies who were glad to take bets. Bets could be placed on baseball, horse racing, football, or anything else that had a questionable outcome. All the accounts for the bookies were kept in ledgers under the name of the person making the bet. How the bookies kept up with it, I don't know, but all the bets were booked under false names. Most everyone went by a pet name and that name stuck.

On one occasion, the gang informer in the City Government did not get word of a 10:00 p.m. raid by the police on this establishment. The gamblers present jumped out of windows, ran out doors, and hid under tables. Cops were everywhere. They broke the slot machines with axes. They chopped up the card tables, though those could easily be replaced. They weren't interested in the petty gamblers, however, all the betting money on the tables mysteriously disappeared. Cops' pockets were bulging but nothing was said. The main target for the raid was to secure the main book where the bets were kept. This way the law thought that they could nail the top bosses and their customers.

Once the ledger was found the police vacated the club. They hurried back to the police station where they turned the precious book over to the City Prosecutor. When the ledger was opened it was found that the entries were made to unidentifiable persons. For example, there was $100 owed by "Possum," $250 owed by "Stinky," $85 owed by "Bones," and $154 owed by "Hatchet." There were no actual names, nor any addresses. There was no way for the prosecutor to go after crazy names with no personal identification. The ledger was completely useless to anyone but the bookies. Since the bookmakers had no record of the debts of the gamblers, they had to rely on honesty. Believe it or not, there was a great sense of honesty and loyalty among the people who frequented these establishments. The word was put out that anyone who was in debt to the bookies could reduce their bills by one half and report their new debt balance to the bookmakers. All but a very few complied with this request. The bookies pretty much knew the people that didn't comply and those were never allowed to place any more wagers at that club, or at any of the clubs that were under the control of this group. Other than the bookies losing a little money, the only thing that happened due to this raid was that the police had to live with a little pie on their faces.

Another illegal activity was the creation of an organization to send love letters to inmates of various prisons. They would pose as women telling the inmates that they would wait for them until their release. The sham would send pictures of lovely ladies to the prisoners and ask them to send money to help support the lady until the inmate got out of jail. Once they got the prisoners hooked, they would begin asking for extra money for their sick mother or to help with a friend in need.

With all these activities, money began flowing in large amounts. Special arrangements had to be made for the securing of such large sums. A special vault was installed in one of the businessmen's offices. Not surprisingly, everyone wanted to get their hands on the money. Arguments escalated among the business partners to a point where the two Biloxi men decided to part ways. This would have been all well and good except the money in the vault suddenly disappeared. The Biloxi men realized that there were bosses higher up that had to be answered to. These bosses would certainly not like to hear that their money had disappeared, no matter what the reason.

Because of fear of the bosses, the Biloxi men began blaming each other. They pointed fingers and called each other names. Finally the higher ups decided to believe one of the men. His story seemed to be more on the up and up.

A hit man was dispersed to deal with the man who was not believed. This part of the drama was quickly over. The businessman and his wife were both killed, mob style, with 22 bullets placed in both of their skulls. The hit man was identified and arrested and the trial of the entire incident began. Witnesses were called and many people testified. Nobody really knew exactly what they were testifying about. The underlying scam was uncovered and the other businessman was arrested and brought to justice. I guess the law was looking for all who were involved in the entire illegal act. A few people were sentenced to jail sentences. Several of the concerned people walked free because nothing could be proven against them. The stolen money was never recovered, but someone probably lived happily ever after.

CHAPTER FOUR

Although there were many local activities that either broke, or closely skirted the law, Biloxi and the Gulf Coast was an ideal place to live. The people were extremely friendly and would generally go out of their way to render assistance to anyone in need. There were a few really rich residents, but most of the people found themselves stuck right in the center of the middle class. Most everyone drove a Chevy or a Ford and the dress was always casual. During Mardi Gras, people who belonged to Carnival organizations would dress up in their finest and attend balls and other glamorous activities. During the Mardi Gras parades, the dress turned back to either costumes or what was known as "Coast Casual."

Over 25 miles of white sand beach stretched along the three counties of the Mississippi Gulf Coast, attracting many tourists. Several large hotels sprang up along Highway 90 where the visiting partygoers found plenty of entertainment. Besides the occasional floating craps game at various hotels or other smaller gambling joints, visitors were always welcomed to the large clubs with their big-name entertainers.

Sunbathing during the day and then partying all night were the normal activities of most of the guests. It was not difficult to find many swollen and bloodshot eyes from lack of sleep and consumption of alcohol. Many historic sites were available along the Coast for visitors to enjoy, and often they would venture to the close-by cities of New Orleans and Mobile.

The hotels and clubs popping up created many jobs for the residents. There was very little unemployment and few were found asking for handouts. The local schools were well-funded and the city created parks and recreation departments. Keesler Air Force Base was located right in the middle of the city's activities. Many airmen came in and out of Keesler, where they received extensive training in radar, electronics, aircraft mechanics, and several other professional fields. Keesler was known as one of the best and largest medical centers in the U.S. Air force. For this reason, and because shopping for food and other necessities was readily available to them, many servicemen returned here to retire.

During foreign military conflicts, many beginning pilots were trained at Keesler, creating considerable noise from the airplanes taking off and landing. Occasionally a pilot would ditch his plane in the shallow waters of the Gulf of Mexico. The plane and pilot were quickly retrieved, creating an interesting sight for locals.

Directly north of the Coast were miles of wooded land covered with longleaf pine. Here several sawmills and a paper mill had owners looking to purchase the pines. Several of the bosses purchased acres of this timber land. Their proximity to the Coast and isolation made these areas ideal for hiding their criminal activities. They developed one of these 300-acre land purchases into a hunting club and firing range. On this site they constructed a well secured fancy hunting club cottage for the entertainment of visiting high-rollers, out of sight of local traffic. Special guests knew there would be a high stakes card game, plenty of booze, and an adequate number of lovely ladies to go around.

As sections of the property became cleared by selling the pine trees to loggers, a helicopter landing pad was built to use for drug transfer, soon becoming the hub of drug traffic for the entire area. Once they started shipments to and from Mexico and Central America, it became a major drug trafficking site for some of the national drug cartels.

Because of the large amounts of drugs passing through, many people got wind of it, including the FBI who raided the site. It took a couple of years to complete the FBI investigations and conduct the court trial proceedings. Drug dealers, local police and sheriffs, state officials, and national drug kingpins were arrested and charged with trafficking.

The only person not charged with this crime was the kingpin of the entire operation, who happened to be in the hospital on the day of the raid. Because of the lack of evidence, he was never indicted for his involvement in this, or any other illicit operation. This close call with the law scared him enough to have him quietly slip away and out of the many activities of the syndicate. Although he was not arrested, he was now completely out of the picture. The property was sold to a logging company who removed most of the trees and then sold the land for a large profit to the highway department.

    For some reason the FBI never wanted to delve into the other activities of organized crime on the Coast which continued to flourish. Some believed this was due to the widespread connections the local Mafioso group had, even in Washington. Several very powerful congressmen came from Mississippi and their families had connections to local "businessmen."

CHAPTER FIVE

Girls, Girls, Girls. The Coast had no shortage of beautiful, desirable ladies available to be hired by the local clubs. They worked as waitresses, bartenders, striptease dancers, and prostitutes. Seldom did any of the ladies move from one employer to another. The bosses knew that a really sexy and personable bartender was a gem and they wanted her to stay right there.

The strippers and pole dancers were ladies who enjoyed exhibiting themselves. They knew how to work the crowd and how to get the most money from the patrons. These ladies would not have switched jobs with any of the other girls, even if they had been asked. No one ever would ask them to, because they were too valuable as dancers to be taken from their jobs. Patrons often returned to the same club just to see a particular girl, or group of girls, perform. The men who were patrons could have any thoughts they pleased, but these ladies were not to be touched or hassled in any way.

    The prostitutes were a completely different breed. Most of the time one could not tell if a lady was a professional or not. They carried themselves very well and were always clean and well dressed. The only time any of these ladies-of-the-night were ill-treated was when they would go off to work with some sleaze of a pimp. These pimps had no concern for the welfare of the girls that worked for them. They were only interested in the money that they could produce. The classier ladies would always want to maintain a position with the bosses of larger establishments.

When the prostitution demand became extremely great, the various clubs would have to hire an overseer to manage the girls. He would take calls and schedule for the ladies to go to various hotels. Some of the joints had back rooms where the women could take their clients who came into the club. The overseer would keep up with the activities of each girl and pay her and the boss accordingly.

One time these ladies turned out to be valuable in the drug industry too. Large shipments of marijuana journeyed from Jamaica to the Tampa Port. To avoid confrontations with the shippers and dealers, the drug lords would send bodyguards to collect the load from the ships. Sometime this arrangement worked and sometimes not. One of the bosses decided to try something a little different. Rather than send the muscles down for the delivery, he chose three of his top prostitutes. They were instructed to go and be friendly with the deliverers of the stash. They were to sidestep any and all antagonistic confrontations, settling any disagreements with their charm and their bodies.

    The ladies went to Tampa where they met the sales agents and made all arrangements for their return to Biloxi with the marijuana. They had been sent to pick up 1,000 pounds of weed, however, due to their charms they returned with 1,400 pounds of sellable drugs for the same amount of money. The Boss was ecstatic. As you can imagine, he paid the ladies very well for their time and efforts. He made up his mind that no more bullies would be sent for drug deliveries and pickups. These ladies had secured themselves a new and prosperous side job. The next delivery was made by the same ladies except this time the bosses went with them. They all cruised down on a 54-foot sports fisher/pleasure boat. I hear that the trip was enjoyed by all.

Soon the Coast Guard caught onto the boat trafficking and they began to monitor the movement of boats across the Gulf. Large, slower boats were usually not targeted as drug runners. One summer Biloxi was flooded with 50-pound, plastic wrapped bags of marijuana that floated up onto the shores. A large pleasure boat had come from Tampa to right inside of our barrier islands and dropped over 100 bales of grass. This stash was wrapped to be watertight and it floated in the Gulf. For the next several days local fishermen and beachcombers scrounged for the floating and washed up bales. The bosses let it be known they'd pay $100 for every bale turned in to them. There would also be retribution for anyone who found a bale and not turned it in. As I recall, there was only one boat that was burned and sunk because of the lack of the captain's understanding of the drug trade and its members. All but four of the original bales of marijuana were recovered. I thought that this was amazing. It was possible that some of it drifted into the

Louisiana marsh and was lost forever. Maybe some Cajun fishermen had a very happy day fishing. Who knows?

CHAPTER SIX

As time progressed, so did the technology and techniques of the operations of the various clubs. The music sound systems became more sophisticated and the quality of entertainers continued to improve. One-armed-bandit slot machines were replaced with automatic operating units. Licenses were required for all clubs and club owners, and even ladies-of-the-night. It went so far as to require the parking lots of the individual clubs to be properly striped. Where would it all end? Would an honest crook no longer be able to make a decent living? Was all illicit activities really going to be brought to a screeching halt?

There were still gambling halls and private games being conducted. Visitors still knew that the Coast would be able to provide for their entertainment and pleasure, wants and needs. Where there was a demand for drugs, prostitution, strippers, and gambling, there would always be someone there to provide. Traveling comedians and comedy shows continued to circulate through the various clubs. Restaurant owners made upgrades to their eateries and hired big-name chefs to prepare expensive gourmet dishes.

The organized gaming promoters wanted Biloxi to become a Mecca for gaming throughout the entire south with legalized gaming. The organizers wanted to attract large casinos to come to the Coast, like those in Las Vegas. They decided to begin the process of having the state vote to legalize gambling. Along with legalized gambling, there had to be a gaming commission which would take much of the power out of the hands of the club owners and bosses.

The organized Coast promoters of gaming knew how to get the acceptance of the state legislators. They set up large parties for the officials with huge quantities of liquor and food, including boiled and fried shrimp, gumbo, crab stew, turtle soup, oysters on the half shell, and other Coast delicacies. Special working ladies were trained to mingle with important people and persuade them to think the way the bosses wanted them to think. Sometimes these girls were useful for providing compromising pictures of the lawmakers. These weren't necessary blackmail ... just wouldn't it have been a pity if some of these revealing pictures had been released for public viewing? No matter what the means were, the effect was what the Coast bosses wanted, a State bill passed the Senate and was placed on a public ballot.

The bosses spent millions on advertising and promoting of the gambling bill. Promotions included TV ads, radio ads, billboards, and small and large town meetings to insure the passage of the gaming bill by the State voters. Although expensive, the bosses knew it would be well worth it.

The owners of the established Coast clubs worried that if big casinos came, the smaller clubs would be left out. These owners held meetings with heated arguments, with great difficulty developing trust in one another since they knew they were all crooked, or at least questionable, business dealers.

In order to appease these current owners, money from the sale and lease of the properties where the new casinos would be built was to be divided among the already established proprietors of the local clubs. Although the new casinos would be taking away business from some of the local clubs, the owners of the already established businesses would reap some reward from the future gaming business. In return for the wealthy property owners sharing with the bosses, the bosses would assure the property owners that they would see to getting the gaming bill passed through the State Senate. The bosses would then call in favors from the Vegas bosses and guarantee that there would be first-class casinos established in Biloxi.

There was just one tiny hitch to these plans for establishing the casinos. The Mississippi legislature, in order to pacify the more conservative voters, put a stipulation on the future casinos. They passed a gaming bill that required that all casinos had to be located on floating structures. The Mississippi tidelands would require leases for the Gulf bottoms, over which the casinos resided. There were obviously some of the crooks from the joints on the Coast that had been elected to State governmental positions. They knew how to keep the ball in their court and get all that they could for the state and for themselves.

Piers beefed up, channels dredged, and support pilings placed in preparation of the new gambling boats, strong enough to hold even during a hurricane. The first gambling boat to arrive in Biloxi was the Capri, named for an island just off of Biloxi that housed the first gambling establishment back in the 1920s. The island mysteriously sank into the Gulf and the popular attraction had never been rebuilt.

When the Capri gambling boat first opened, there were lines of guests that waited outside for a chance to view it. Because of fire regulations, only a certain number of guests could be allowed on at any one time. As guests came off, other guests would go on. To say that the boat was extremely crowded would be a major understatement.

    Next to come to Biloxi was a Riverboat stern wheeler. It was decked out with old steamboat decor, complete with a banjo player that would greet the guests. This boat was moored on a pier in the area of the old Buena Vista hotel. Like the other first gaming boats, it was extremely smoky and crowded. People stood in lines for hours waiting to get a chance to go aboard and view the newcomer.

Down the beach, farther to the west, was another large boat called "The Treasure Bay." This boat was designed like an old pirate ship. The waitresses and dealers were dressed in swashbuckling garb, which matched the internal decorations of the boat. Everything seemed to be first class.

    These casino boats had to be designed so they could be disconnected from their moorings and taken to a safe location in the case of seriously inclimite weather, such as a hurricane. Soon it was discovered that it would be more dangerous to move these vessels than to just secure them, or sink them in the shallow waters. The largest fear was that they would damage bridges and other structures while the boats were being moved. These bridges were vital to the movement and evacuation of the Coastal residents. They certainly did not need to be put out of function at this strategic time.

Someone came up with the idea that the boats should have to go out to federal waters before they would be allowed to conduct gambling. This was the accepted procedure for about six months. After that, it was decided that Biloxi was not like other areas in the US who made their boats go into federal waters. The boats were perfectly well accepted being left alone. These permanent locations caused for much less confusion and strife for law enforcement personnel, as well as for the guests.

CHAPTER SEVEN

In 2005 along came Hurricane Katrina, the most destructive hurricane to hit the Gulf Coast in recorded history. It destroyed property from New Orleans to the Alabama State line. Western Mississippi caught the most damage because of the extensive tidal waves and rising waters. Some of the property there was only five or six feet above sea level. In places, Katrina brought 28 to 30-foot tidal surges. This was enough water to cover most of the existing buildings along the entire Coast for half a mile inland.

The designers of the floating casinos had not planned for such a terrific storm.

The moorings and piers let go of their prize cargos and the casino boats washed up onto the beaches, highways and shores of the Gulf Coast. When the waters receded, some of the casinos were unrecognizable because of the extensive damage done to them. One of the casino boats ended up smack in the middle of Highway 90, another on top of a hotel. The ruined structures had to be dismantled in order to remove them from blocking traffic. Coins and gambling chips were scattered all over the beaches. Looters made away with money and property that had been washed out of the casinos. However, most locals recognized that with so much suffering and destruction, it was appropriate to return all possessions to their original owners, even sacks of money!

It took six months of cleanup before the first casino reopened. The ones furthest from the water had suffered the least damage, and with creditors demanding return on their large investments a hurricane was no excuse for not reopening. Every day the facility stayed shut down, more money was lost for the owners and directors.

The State realized how much money they had been receiving from taxing the casinos. They also wanted to see the casinos reopened as quickly as possible. The state legislature passed a bill stating that casinos would no longer be required to build on waterways or over natural tidal water. They could build within a certain distance from the mean tide location along the beach. Soon casinos began to be built on land, near the beach and waterways. They still had to be close to the water of rivers or the Gulf. Stipulations placed on the casinos stated that they had to construct a certain number of hotel rooms for the guests of their establishments. This was a great incentive for more hotel rooms to be created with new lodging for more visiting guests.

Soon large casinos with beautiful hotels sprung up along the beach and bays. The only restriction to their growth was the number and presence of investors. It was difficult to attract multimillion-dollar investors if they found that the casino and hotel market was already overbuilt. Rather than seeing haphazard buildings being constructed, the investors and gaming commission researched where and how many of the casinos would be placed.

The entire Mississippi Gulf Coast, including Louisiana, are now spotted with lovely hotels and casinos. Large name restaurants have come into the area associated with the gaming locations. Spas, pools, and marinas all profit from being in this rapidly growing economy.

The Coast has become the Mecca for tourism that the bosses wanted from the very start. Although much of the leadership has been taken out of the hands of the local bosses, organized alcohol and gambling has built the Mississippi Gulf Coast into a real vacationers' paradise and a true destination for all visitors, adults and children alike.

www.ingramcontent.com/pod-product-compliance
Lightning Source LLC
Chambersburg PA
CBHW051712040426
42446CB00008B/838